The Amazing HUMAN MACHINE

written by Lori C. Froeb
reviewed by Mansoor Ahmad, MD, PhD

Reader's Digest Children's Books

New York, New York • Montréal, Québec • Bath, United Kingdom

*D*id you ever stop to think about how amazing your body is? Every minute, it is working to keep you growing, moving, thinking, and feeling. Thousands of parts all operate together like a living machine—more complex than any machine on Earth. Inside this book you will learn about many of the systems that make up your body— your skeleton, muscles, nerves, organs, and more. Let's see what makes your amazing body tick!

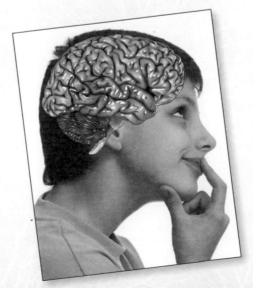

The Amazing Human Machine

Contents

It Starts with Cells

Every part of your body has something very small in common—**cells**. You need a microscope to see them, but don't let their size fool you. When millions of cells get together, they form your skin, bones, brain, and organs. Your body has approximately 75 trillion cells total and every single one of them is a living factory that is busy 24 hours a day.

Cells are the smallest units of life. Humans have over 200 different kinds and each kind has its own special job to do. Some form **tissues** like bone, skin, taste buds, or eyes. Others make and secrete important materials like **hormones**, sweat, earwax, or **saliva**! Very special cells—sperm in men and eggs in women—exist only to create a new human!

Secret Lives of Cells

Skin cells live up to one month. Red blood cells live about 120 days. Liver cells live 5–6 months. Nerve cells can live for more than 100 years!

Cell Shapes

A cell's shape can give clues to what its job is. Take a look at these cell superstars!

Stellar Cells

There are about the same number of nerve cells in the human brain as there are stars in the Milky Way!

Red Blood Cell

The round, smooth, donutlike shape of these cells helps them move easily through the **blood vessels** in the body.

Bone Cell

This cell's fingerlike edges help it to connect and communicate with surrounding bone cells to make strong bones.

Muscle Cell

Muscle cells have the ability to contract (get shorter) and relax (get longer). These are heart muscle cells and they are what make your heart beat.

Nerve Cell

Nerve cells are long and thin and use chemicals and a type of electric charge to carry messages to other cells in the body. Some can be several feet long!

Sperm Cell and Egg Cell

The sperm cell's long tail is used to swim to the egg cell. When an egg and sperm cell meet, a baby begins to form.

The Skin You're In

Skin is the body's largest and heaviest **organ**. It has several very important jobs to do. Its most important job is to keep **germs** and other harmful things out of your body. The skin also helps keep your body temperature from getting too hot or too cold, keeps the correct amount of moisture inside your tissues, and gives you your sense of touch! Skin also has the unique ability to make vitamin D when it absorbs sunlight.

Without skin, this girl's body would have no way to keep all the water out while she swims.

You're Blushing!

Humans are the only animals that blush with emotion. When a person feels anger or embarrassment, blood rushes to the surface of the skin, turning it red.

Skin Deep

You can't tell that there is much going on by just looking at your skin.

As a matter of fact, the skin surface you see is dead! You have to look underneath to see where all the action takes place. This lower layer is called the dermis and it is where hair grows, sweat is made, and where the nerves are that provide a sense of touch.

This is a cross section of human skin. Let's check it out!

capillaries
These tiny blood vessels bring blood full of **nutrients** and oxygen to feed the skin cells.

hair follicle
This is where hair is made. There is one follicle for each strand of hair. Sometimes two hairs can grow out of one follicle.

muscle
These tiny muscles are called erector pili and they make your hair stand up when you are cold. You get goosebumps when they contract!

epidermis
This is the skin you see. It is constantly being replaced by new cells from underneath as the dead ones flake off.

dermis
The sweat glands, oil glands, hair follicles, and nerve endings live here.

subcutaneous fat
This layer of fat is what helps keep you warm and protected from minor bumps and falls.

nerves
Nerves in the dermis can sense five different things: cold, heat, pain, touch, and pressure. There are specific nerve sensors for each of these things.

sweat gland
These **glands** release sweat constantly to keep your body cool. Sweat comes out of the tiny pores on the surface of your skin.

oil gland
These glands make oil or sebum to help protect your skin from drying out and make it waterproof.

Pigments and Fingerprints

Human skin comes in many different shades—from very dark brown to very pale pink. Why? Skin gets its color from melanin—a **pigment** that some skin cells make. The more melanin the skin makes, the darker it is. Darker skin has more protection from the sun's harmful rays than lighter skin does and occurs more in people who live in hot climates. Melanin is also what gives hair and eyes their color!

When Pigment Is Missing

Rarely, a person is born with no pigment at all. This is called albinism. His skin and hair are white and he may have red or pink eyes. Animals can be albino, too, like this squirrel.

Freckle Fact

Do you have freckles? Blame your melanin! Freckles are spots on the skin where more melanin is being produced.

Take a close look at your fingertips. Are they perfectly smooth? No! Your fingertips are full of ridges and valleys that form patterns that are totally unique to you. No one else on earth has the same fingerprints that you do. You might think that identical twins would have the same fingerprints—but they don't. This is why fingerprints are an important tool detectives use to figure out who was at a crime scene.

Your fingerprints are useful for more than identification—without them you'd have a hard time keeping a tight grip on things with wet or smooth surfaces. The ridges and valleys give your skin more friction to grasp these materials.

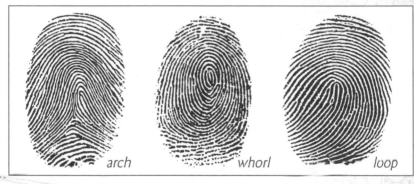

arch   whorl   loop

There are three general fingerprint patterns: arches, whorls, and loops. Your ten fingers may have a variety of these patterns. Additionally, loops and whorls can face left or right. What patterns do you have?

Waterlogged!

This happens when the skin absorbs more water than it can get rid of. The skin soaks up the water and becomes "too big" for your fingertip, so it wrinkles!

Your Fabulous Framework

Your skin protects everything inside your body, but what makes sure you don't slump to the ground like you are made out of jelly? It's your skeleton! Its job is to give your body shape, protect your organs, provide a place for your muscles to attach, and make blood cells.

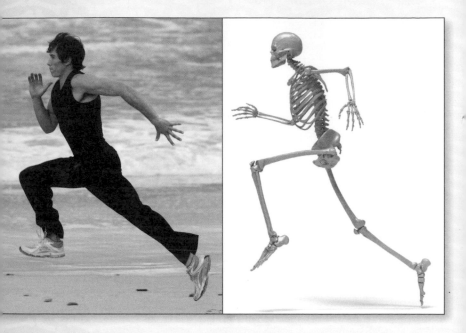

An adult skeleton is made up of 206 bones. Each one is made of a very hard mineral called calcium. The only substance in your body harder than bone is the **enamel** on your teeth. Throughout your whole life, your bones make and remake themselves. Certain cells break the old bone down, while other cells build it up.

The Hard Facts

Your skeleton stores about 98% of all the calcium in your body. If you don't eat enough calcium, your body will take it from your bones. This is why it's important to include dairy, green leafy vegetables, and some nuts in your diet.

The Skeletal System

Here is what an adult human skeleton looks like. When a baby is born, he has over 270 bones, but as he grows the bones fuse together. Once he's an adult, 270 bones have become 206!

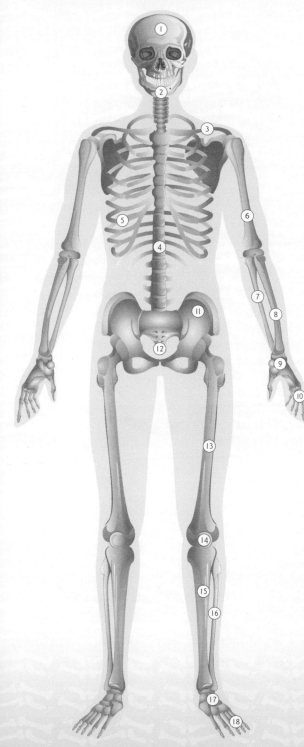

1. **skull**
The 22 bones that make up the skull protect the brain.

2. **mandible**

3. **clavicle**
You might know this as your collarbone.

4. **spine**
The spine is made up of 33 smaller bones called vertebrae.

5. **ribs**
The 24 ribs protect the heart and lungs.

6. **humerus**

7. **ulna**

8. **radius**

9. **carpals**
Eight carpals make up the human wrist.

10. **phalanges**

11. **pelvis**

12. **coccyx**
Also called a tailbone, the coccyx can be made up of 3, 4, or 5 bones.

13. **femur**
This is the longest and heaviest bone in the human body.

14. **patella**
Your patella protects your knee joint.

15. **tibia**

16. **fibula**

17. **tarsals**
Seven tarsals make up the ankle of the human foot.

18. **phalanges**

Bone Tour

Bones are hard and strong, but they are also very light. Look inside a bone, and you'll see that it is made of several different layers.

Dry Bones?

When you think of a bone, you probably imagine a dry, hard object. You might be surprised to learn that almost a quarter of a bone's weight is water!

1. **spongy bone**
It's easy to see how this layer got its name—it looks like a sponge! This layer has many blood vessels.

2. **bone marrow**
The bone marrow's job is to make blood cells—millions of them every second!

3. **compact bone**
This is the strongest layer of bone. It contains many small tubes that hold the bone's blood vessels. This part of the bone is light, but very strong.

4. **periosteum**
The outermost layer of bone is a thin "skin" full of tiny blood vessels that feed the bone.

Baby Bones

When babies are born, most of their skeleton is not bone—it's cartilage. Cartilage is a soft "rubbery" material that is strong, but flexible. Over 20 years or so, most of the cartilage uses calcium to gradually get harder and turn into bone. An adult's skeleton still has some cartilage—it lines the joints and forms the ears and nose!

Connect the Bones

Bones can't bend. But without being able to bend, you wouldn't be able to walk, scratch your head, hold a ball, or touch your toes. This is what around 230 joints in your body are for!

There are several different kinds of joints in your body. Your knee is a hinge joint. It lets your leg bend back and forth. Your neck has pivot joints that let it turn. Your hips and shoulders have ball-and-socket joints that let these limbs move in almost any direction. Some joints—like the ones in your skull—don't move. They keep the bones in your head snug to protect your brain.

hip (ball-and-socket joint)

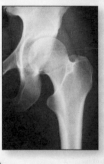

knee (hinge joint)

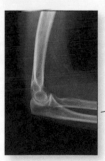

elbow (hinge joint)

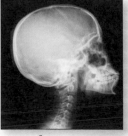

neck (pivot joints)

Joint Effort
When you take one step, you move 62 bones in your pelvis, legs, and feet. When you shrug your shoulders, you move 64 bones from your collarbone to your pinkies!

Mighty Muscles

What makes your muscles mighty? Muscles take energy from the food you eat and turn it into power. They help you blink your eyes, kick a ball, pump blood through your body, take a breath, and even help you digest your food!

There are two kinds of muscles in your body: voluntary and involuntary. Voluntary muscles are the ones that you tell your body to move—your finger muscles, for example. Involuntary muscles are controlled by your brain. Your heart is an involuntary muscle and so are the muscles in your stomach and blood vessels.

Muscular You!

Muscles make up about one third of your body's weight! Your largest muscle is your gluteus maximus—that's the muscle that forms your buttocks. Your smallest muscle is in your ear—it looks like a wisp of cotton.

The Muscular System

Your bones can't move all by themselves. It's a good thing you have more than 600 muscles to do the job! The muscles that help you run, swing a bat, and even smile are called skeletal muscles. They are attached to your skeleton by tough bands called tendons.

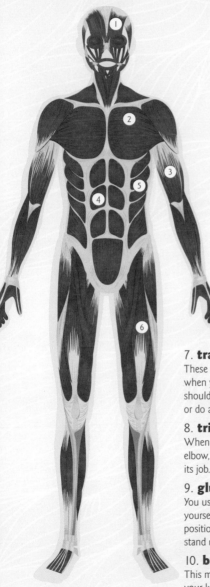

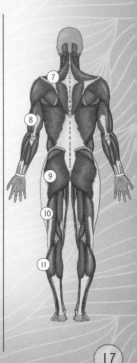

1. frontalis
These muscles let you wrinkle your forehead and raise your eyebrows.

2. pectoralis major
You use this muscle when you arm wrestle or lift something in front of you.

3. biceps
When you tighten a screw, it's your biceps doing the work.

4. rectus abdominus
When you do a sit-up or crunch you are using these muscles.

5. oblique
These muscles help you bend your body, twist back and forth, and bend from side to side.

6. quadriceps
Walking, jumping, squatting, and running are all actions this group of four muscles makes possible.

7. trapezius
These muscles are at work when you shrug your shoulders, throw a ball, or do a pull-up.

8. triceps
When you straighten your elbow, this muscle is doing its job.

9. gluteus maximus
You use this muscle to lift yourself from a squatting position. It also helps you stand up straight.

10. biceps femoris
This muscle is used to bend your knee. It works with your quadriceps to help you walk and run.

11. gastrocnemius
This muscle bends your foot down to help you jump and stand on tiptoe.

Muscle Teams

Skeletal muscles work together in pairs to make your body move. The triceps and biceps are an example of this teamwork. When you want to bend your elbow, your biceps contracts (gets shorter) and the triceps relaxes (gets longer). When you want to straighten your arm, your triceps contracts and your biceps relaxes.

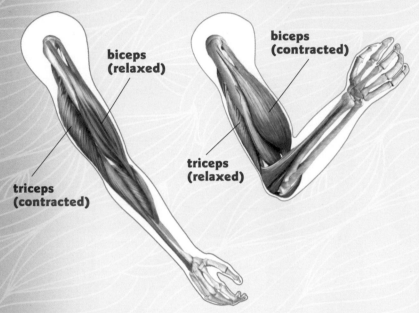

biceps
(relaxed)

biceps
(contracted)

triceps
(relaxed)

triceps
(contracted)

Muscle Power

The more you use your muscles, the bigger and stronger they get. Muscles are made up of many long strands of muscle cells. Bodybuilders perform exercises that use certain muscles over and over again. The more each muscle is used, the thicker the long strands get—making them stand out and look like this:

Make a Face

If you could see through the skin on your face, this is what you'd see. Your face is full of muscles—more than 40 of them! Many of them are attached to the underside of your skin instead of bone. When they contract, they do things like make you smile, scrunch your nose, or raise your eyebrows!

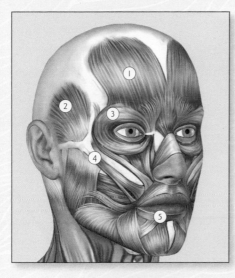

1. **frontalis**
This is the muscle that raises your eyebrows when you are surprised.

2. **temporalis**
Open your mouth wide! You just used this muscle.

3. **orbicularis oculi**
Ready to sleep? This muscle will close your eyelids.

4. **zygomaticus**
To smile, you'll need this muscle.

5. **orbicularis oris**
This muscle controls your lips so you can pucker up.

The muscles in your face are what let you make dozens of expressions!

Smooth Operators

Some of your organs have muscles, too. They are called smooth muscles and work without you even knowing it! When you swallow, muscles in your esophagus (or food tube) contract to push the food down into your stomach. Your bladder, which holds **urine**, is lined with smooth muscle. The muscles are relaxed until you are ready to use the bathroom—then they contract and squeeze the urine out.

A Living Network

How do your muscles know when to move? How do you know something is too hot to touch? How do you hear? Think? Your nervous system is what controls everything your body does. It is like a very complex computer network made of nerves instead of wires. Like a computer, your body even uses a special kind of electricity to send and receive messages.

When you use a computer, your nervous system is hard at work. Without it, you wouldn't be able to see the screen, think about what to write, feel the keyboard, move your fingers to type, or hear your mother calling you for dinner!

On Duty

Even when you are asleep, your nervous system is on duty. It keeps you breathing, lets you turn in your sleep, wakes you up if it detects danger nearby, and creates dreams!

The Nervous System

Your nerves, brain, and spinal cord make up your nervous system. Nerves reach from your brain to your face, ears, nose, and spinal cord. Then they stretch from your spinal cord to every part of your body.

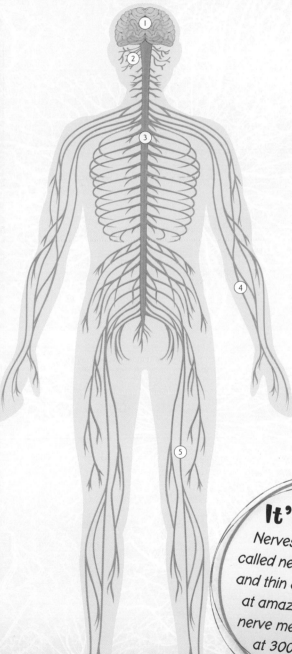

1. brain
Messages are constantly leaving and entering your brain—moving at up to 225 miles per hour!

2. facial nerves
This network of nerves controls the movement of your face and is what lets you feel a kiss on your cheek.

3. spinal cord
The cord is made up of millions of nerve cells and is 17 to 18 inches long in an adult.

4. ulnar nerve
What you might call your "funny bone" is actually a large nerve that runs down your arm on the inside of your elbow.

5. sciatic nerve
This is the longest and thickest nerve in your body. It goes from your lower back all the way down to your foot.

It's Electric!
Nerves are made of cells called neurons. They are long and thin and send messages at amazing speeds—some nerve messages can travel at 300 feet a second!

What Nerve!

When a neuron picks up a message—cold, pain, sound, or other things—it makes a tiny electrical pulse that travels down the cell's thin body. When the pulse gets to the end of the cell, special chemicals let the message "jump" to the neurons nearby. This is how messages quickly get to the spinal cord, and then to the brain.

1. **dendrite**
This is where the cell receives a message.

2. **body**
This is the part of the cell that takes in nutrients to power the cell.

3. **axon**
The message travels from the body toward the end of the axon.

4. **axon terminal**
The message jumps from here to nearby nerve cells.

Neurons look like tiny trees.
Many neurons line up to make nerves.

Senior Citizen Cells!

Nerve cells can live over 100 years, but they can't reproduce like all the other cells in your body. By the time a person is two years old, he already has most of the neurons he will ever have.

The Brain: Command Central

An adult brain weighs about three pounds—less than 2% of the body's weight, but no organ is as complex. The brain takes all the information from the billions of nerves in your body, processes them, and sends commands if needed. It also holds your memories, controls things like breathing and blood pressure, warms and cools your body, and lets you think.

Let's tour your brain!

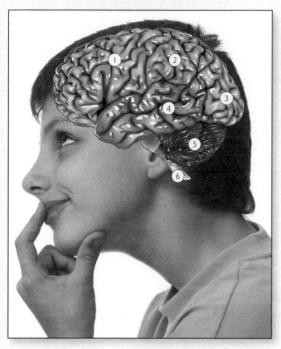

Each area of your brain has a different job to do! The large wrinkly part of your brain is called the cerebrum. It is made mostly (85%) of water!

1. frontal lobe
This area controls thinking, memory, and helps you make decisions.

2. parietal lobe
This area processes sensations and helps you be aware of your body in its surroundings.

3. occipital lobe
This area manages the information coming from your eyes and allows you to see and dream.

4. temporal lobe
Your speech, hearing, and understanding of language comes from this area.

5. cerebellum
Your sense of balance, coordination, and movement is controlled here.

6. brain stem
This area controls your breathing, heart rate, awareness, and food digestion.

The Hungry Brain

Your brain uses a lot of nutrients and oxygen to keep working properly. About 12 gallons of blood an hour rush through the brain to make sure it gets what it needs!

How You See

Look around you. What do you see? Whatever it is, you have your eyes to thank!

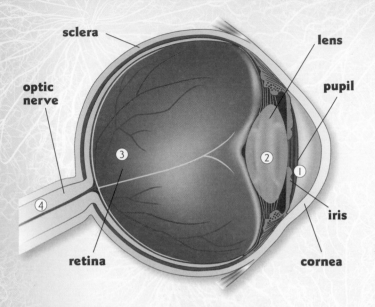

sclera

lens

optic nerve

pupil

③

②

①

④

retina

iris

cornea

This is a cross section of a human eye. An adult eye is about the size of a ping-pong ball and sits in the eye socket—protected all around by the skull.

1. Light bounces off objects and enters the eye through the pupil. This is the dark opening in the middle of your eye.

2. The light passes through the lens. The lens changes shape to focus on objects near and far.

3. The lens focuses the light onto the back of the eye (the **retina**). The retina changes the light into nerve signals that the brain can understand.

4. The optic nerve is wired right into the brain. The nerve signals from the eye travel to the brain at up to 42 miles per hour! Now you're seeing!

Eye Cry

All animals make tears to keep the eye moist and protected. But only humans cry from emotion. The tears you make when you cry are even made of different chemicals than your regular tears.

How You Hear

Just as your eyes collect light for the brain to translate into images, your ears collect vibrations for the brain to translate into sound.

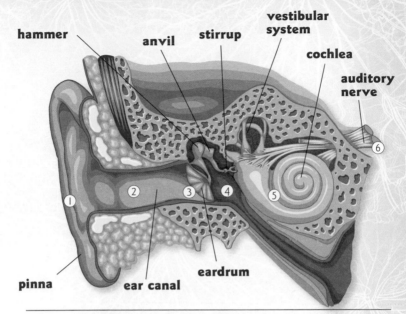

If you could look inside your head past your outer ear, this is what you'd see. The smallest bones in your body—the hammer, anvil, and stirrup—are part of your hearing system.

1. Your outer ear, or pinna, collects sound vibrations.

2. The sound enters the ear canal.

3. The sound hits the eardrum and makes it vibrate.

4. The vibrating eardrum makes three tiny ear bones move.

5. The bones' vibrations pass on to the **cochlea**. Inside the cochlea, microscopic hairs move and make nerve signals.

6. The auditory nerve takes these signals to the brain, which then tells you what you heard!

Balancing Act

The vestibular system is what helps you keep your balance. It is full of fluid that is level when you are standing straight. When the fluid moves, the brain uses the information to make adjustments to your body to keep it from falling over.

How You Taste

What is your favorite food? How does it taste? How do you know? Your tongue is tasting central. If you look closely at its surface you will see that it is covered in tiny bumps called **papillae**. Inside each papilla are your taste buds. These bunches of cells collect **molecules** from the food you eat and send signals to the brain—which, in turn, tells you what you are tasting!

sweet ●

● bitter

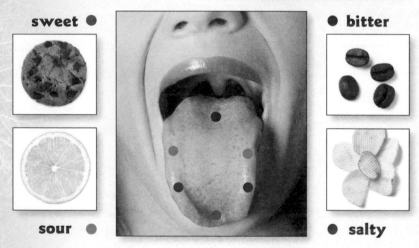

sour ●

● salty

Each of your taste buds mainly detects one basic taste (sweet, sour, bitter, salty). Some parts of the tongue have more buds of one type. Those areas are more sensitive to that taste than others.

Tongues Are Terrific!

About 16 muscles make up your tongue. Besides tasting, it forms sound, moves food around your mouth, and guards your throat to keep you from choking on objects. Some people can curl their tongues like this girl. A person can't learn to do this— you are either born with the ability or not.

How You Smell

Your nose is more than just a fancy facial feature—it is the reason you can smell cookies baking or the perfume your mom wears. Deep inside your nose is a patch of about 10 million nerve cells that have small hairs called **cilia**. These cells pick up scent molecules and send a message to the brain. The brain puts together thousands of these messages to decide what you are smelling!

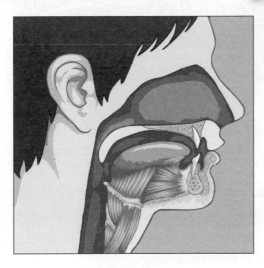

*The lining of your nose is thin and moist. Called the **mucous membrane**, this lining makes **mucus**—otherwise known as snot. Scent molecules dissolve in mucus. This makes them easier to detect!*

Sneeze, Please!

Mucus is great at keeping things like dust, pollen, and other things out of your body. If something does get in, you may sneeze to get rid of it. During a sneeze, particles leave your nose at up to 100 miles per hour!

Go with the Flow

Every cell in the body needs a regular supply of oxygen and **nutrients** to keep working. Each cell also needs a way to get rid of waste products. That's a lot of cells that need constant attention! Good thing your body is equipped with a kind of superhighway that can do the job—your cardiovascular system!

The blood contains everything the body's cells need. But the blood isn't just floating around your organs and tissues—it is contained in tubes called blood vessels. Large vessels branch off into smaller and smaller vessels until they are almost too small to see. Veins, arteries, and capillaries are all blood vessels.

Very Small Vessels

The smallest vessels in your body are called capillaries. Some are so tiny that your red blood cells must line up in single file to get through!

The Cardiovascular System

Up to 60,000 miles of blood vessels make up this body system! Blood is kept moving through the whole body as the heart pumps. In this diagram, veins are blue and arteries are red.

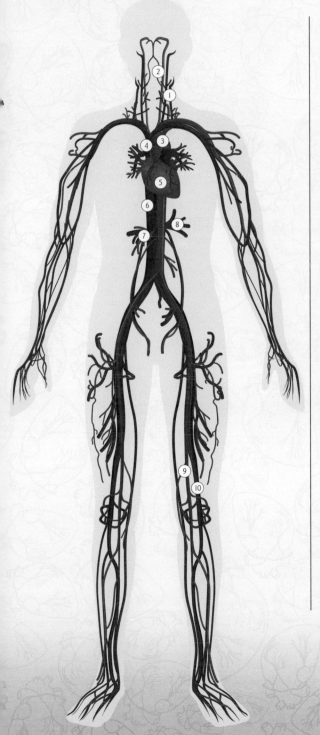

1. **jugular vein**
Takes blood from the brain and head back to the heart through the superior vena cava.

2. **carotid artery**
Brings nutrients and oxygen-rich blood to the brain and head.

3. **aorta**
Largest artery in the body that carries blood with fresh oxygen away from the heart.

4. **superior vena cava**
A large vein that carries blood that needs oxygen from the head and arms to the heart.

5. **heart**
The heart pumps to keep the blood moving through the entire system.

6. **inferior vena cava**
Largest vein in the body that carries blood that needs oxygen from the legs to the heart.

7. **renal artery**
Carries blood to the kidneys where it is filtered to remove waste.

8. **renal vein**
Carries blood away from the kidneys.

9. **femoral artery**

10. **femoral vein**

The Heart of the Matter

Your heart is a muscle that never rests. Slightly bigger than your fist, this organ keeps blood moving nonstop through your body by squeezing it through four chambers. Every time your heart beats, you can feel a wave of pressure in your larger arteries. This is what you feel in your wrist or neck when you check your pulse! A child's heart rate is about 90 beats a minute while an adult's is about 70 beats a minute.

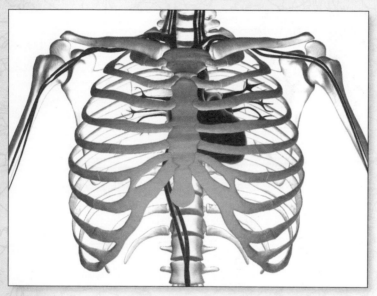

Your heart is protected by your rib cage and sits just to the left of the center of your chest.

Your brain controls how fast your heart beats without you thinking about it. When you exercise, your muscles need more oxygen and nutrients, so your brain tells your heart to beat faster. When you are sleeping, your body needs less of these things and your heart slows down.

Quick Trip!

Count 60 seconds. That's about how long it takes blood from your heart to travel all the way down to the tips of your toes and back up to your heart again!

Your Heart

The heart is a pump. Blood that needs oxygen comes into the right side of the heart through the vena cava and is pumped to the lungs. Blood that has just picked up fresh oxygen from the lungs enters the left side of the heart through the **pulmonary** veins and goes to the rest of the body through the aorta.

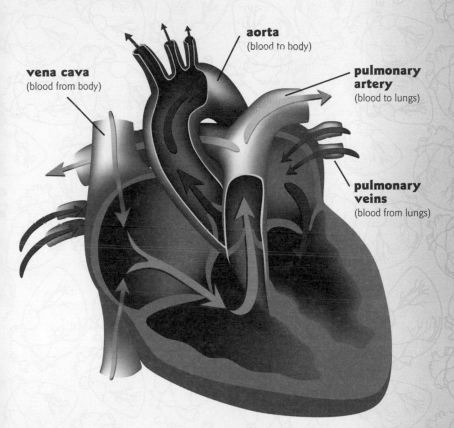

vena cava
(blood from body)

aorta
(blood to body)

pulmonary artery
(blood to lungs)

pulmonary veins
(blood from lungs)

The arrows are showing how blood moves in and out of the heart. Blood that comes into the heart from your lungs is bright red because it is full of oxygen. The blood that comes into the heart from the rest of your body is dark red because all the oxygen has been given to your cells.

Blood Business

Your cardiovascular system is very good at making sure your blood keeps moving. But what *is* blood? Blood is what carries life-giving oxygen and nutrients to your body. It also takes waste products like carbon dioxide away. It contains your body's germ defense and repair systems. Humans have up to a gallon and a half of blood in their bodies.

plasma
Made mostly of water, plasma carries the blood cells, hormones, nutrients, and waste products through the body. More than half of blood is plasma.

red blood cell
There are 700 red cells for every one white cell. They have a **protein** called **hemoglobin** that carries oxygen and makes them appear red. About 45% of blood is red cells.

platelet
These "sticky" cell pieces rush to a bleeding injury and stick together to plug up the wound and stop the bleeding.

monocyte
A type of white blood cell that finds **bacteria** and **viruses** in the body. The monocyte surrounds a germ and destroys it. This is called **phagocytosis**.

lymphocyte
These special cells make something called **antibodies**. Antibodies are proteins that recognize specific germs and destroy them. These cells have a good memory. If they encounter the same germ again they are much faster at eliminating it.

Platelet Power!
All the platelets in your body wouldn't even fill two teaspoons, but you have billions of them!

Blood to the Rescue!

Anytime there is a break in your skin, germs and bacteria have a way to get into your body to cause infections. Some infections can be dangerous enough to kill you. Fortunately, your body has a very effective way of dealing with the situation. So what happens when you get a cut or scrape? Let's find out!

When the skin is injured, cells in that area send out signals to let your body know there is a problem.

Immediately, platelets collect in the injured area and start to plug up the wound. A stringlike material called **fibrin** traps red cells and platelets around the wound and forms a clot.

White blood cells also rush to the scene to destroy any germs or bacteria that may be getting into the body. You can sometimes see them—pus is made up of white cells and plasma.

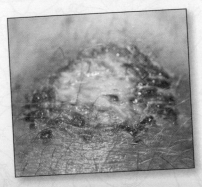

Eventually, the clot dries up and forms a scab. Under the protection of the scab, the skin wound slowly heals as your body makes new cells to replace the damaged ones. Once the repair is finished, the scab falls off.

Attack Back!

Have you ever been sick and noticed swollen glands in your neck? Or had sore tonsils? Then you've felt your lymphatic system at work! Like your cardiovascular system, your lymphatic system is made of vessels. But instead of blood, these vessels are full of lymph—a fluid like plasma that contains lots of white blood cells.

Scattered all throughout your body are tiny little germ filters called lymph nodes. As the lymph passes through the nodes, they filter out germs. Each node is also full of lymphocytes. When they get a message about a germ inside the body, the lymphocytes quickly get to work multiplying and making the antibodies to take care of it. Nodes near the site of the infection may swell as a result of the effort.

Immune System Attack!

Sometimes the body overreacts to things that are normally harmless—things like pollen, peanuts, or cat hair. What is the result? Allergies. Often, a person with allergies will have many of the same symptoms as when their body is fighting a cold— a sore throat, sneezing, and a stuffed nose.

The Lymphatic System

Lymph nodes and vessels aren't the only things that make up your lymphatic system. It also contains a couple of organs—the thymus and spleen. Your lymphatic system and white cells in your blood are what make up your immune system—your body's disease-fighting arsenal.

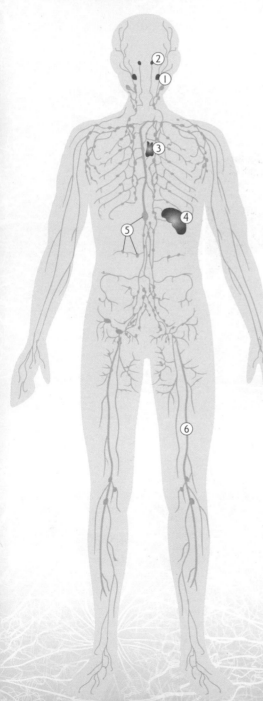

1. tonsil
You have two tonsils in your throat. They are your body's first line of defense against viruses and bacteria that you inhale or eat.

2. adenoids
A type of tonsil between your nose and throat, adenoids usually are not active after the age of three or so.

3. thymus
This small, fatty organ takes your white cells from your bone marrow and "trains" them to become special "T-cells" that make antibodies for specific germs. Then it releases them into the bloodstream.

4. spleen
Up to half of the monocytes in your body are stored here. The spleen also makes antibodies to fight infection and keeps about a cup of blood in storage that it can release in case of emergency.

5. lymph nodes
There are between 500 and 600 nodes in your body.

6. lymph vessels

Take a Breather

Your body needs a constant supply of oxygen to survive. The brain in particular can't be without it for more than 5 minutes before it starts to die. Your respiratory system takes the air you breathe and makes it available to your red blood cells for transport around the body.

The process starts when you breathe in. A flat muscle beneath your lungs called the diaphragm moves down and causes air to be sucked into your nose and/or mouth and down your trachea (or windpipe). Tiny cilia in your trachea trap any dust or dirt in the air and, together with mucus, move the dirt up and out of your body.

Breathing for Fun

Normal breathing is involuntary, but you can control it when you need to—like when you are playing an instrument or blowing out candles.

While resting, you breathe in and out about 18 times a minute. This adds up—every day, you breathe around 3,500 gallons of air into your lungs—enough to fill about 875 balloons!

The Respiratory System

The trachea branches into two tubes called bronchi—each leads to one lung. The bronchi branch into smaller and smaller tubes called bronchioles. At the ends of the smallest bronchioles are alveoli—tiny air sacs that are surrounded by capillaries. The red blood cells pick up the oxygen from the alveoli and take it to every cell in your body! You're breathing!

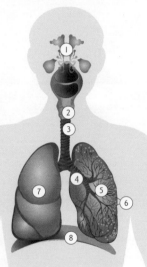

1. **sinuses**
The sinuses add moisture and warmth to the air you breathe in.

2. **vocal cords**
When you speak, air moves past these folds of tissue and makes them vibrate to produce sound—your voice.

3. **trachea**

4. **bronchus**
You have two bronchi.

5. **bronchioles**
Your smallest bronchioles are about the same thickness as a human hair.

6. **alveoli**
Your lungs have about 500 *million* alveoli inside!

7. **lung**
Your right lung has three sections, or lobes, while your left lung has two. It is smaller to make room for your heart.

8. **diaphragm**

Hic!

Sometimes the diaphragm may contract and pull down abruptly. Air is quickly sucked in and the vocal cords close to prevent too much air from getting into the lungs. What's happening? A hiccup!

Food for Fuel!

Your body needs energy to do everything from thinking to breathing, from moving to repairing itself. Where does this energy come from? The food you eat! Your digestive system's job is to break down food into materials the body can use. Proteins, fats, carbohydrates, and vitamins all come from food, and each is used in different ways.

Carbohydrates are your body's main energy source. Carbohydrates are sugars that are easy for the body to use as energy. Bread, rice, grains, potatoes, and pasta all contain carbohydrates.

Protein is used for body growth and repair. The body uses protein to build muscle, make hair and nails, and repair skin. Meat, fish, beans, and dairy products all have protein.

Fat is an important part of a person's diet. In reasonable amounts, fat helps the body use vitamins. It also helps keep nerves and the cells healthy. Cheese, butter, oil, and nuts all have fat.

Vitamins and minerals help keep your body working properly. Some help make bones strong. Others help you heal. And some are used to help your body protect itself from germs. Most foods have a variety of vitamins and minerals.

Food=Energy

Food energy is measured in calories. A child needs about 1,500 calories a day and an adult needs between 2,000 and 2,500.

The Digestive System

Your digestive system is very good at taking food and turning it into things your body can use. It also makes sure that the things your body doesn't use—waste—leaves the body efficiently. Check out where all this food-to-fuel action takes place!

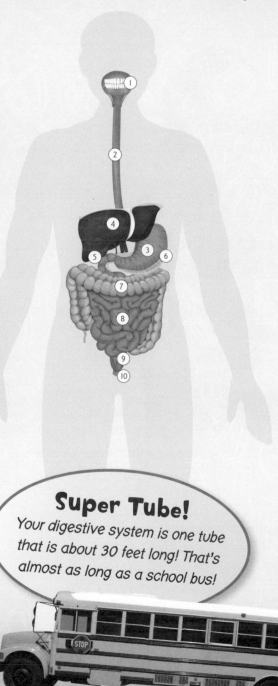

1. **mouth**
Digestion begins here when saliva mixes with the food you eat.

2. **esophagus**

3. **stomach**
Your stomach is about as big as your fist, but it can stretch a lot.

4. **liver**
This is your body's biggest gland and it has hundreds of jobs—from recycling blood cells to making bile that digests fats.

5. **gallbladder**
This small organ stores and releases bile.

6. **pancreas**
This gland makes **insulin** to help your body use sugar. It also makes **enzymes** to break down food in the small intestine.

7. **large intestine**
Extra water from digested food is absorbed back into the body as it moves through. The large intestine also contains more than 700 species of bacteria that provide vitamins for the body.

8. **small intestine**
Over 18 feet long, this intestine is not so small.

9. **rectum**

10. **anus**

Super Tube!

Your digestive system is one tube that is about 30 feet long! That's almost as long as a school bus!

STOP

39

Down the Hatch!

It takes two to three days for food to go from your mouth to your anus. What happens to it along the way? Food is moved through your digestive tract by strong muscle contractions. Slimy mucus helps it travel smoothly through all the twists, turns, and folds. It's a wild ride!

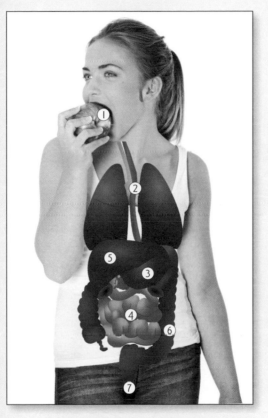

1. The teeth mash the food and mix it with saliva. The mashed food forms a bolus and is swallowed.
2. Muscle contractions in the esophagus move the bolus to the stomach.
3. The stomach squeezes and churns to mix the bolus with digestive juices that turn the food into a soup called chyme.
4. Chyme reaches the small intestine where nutrients are absorbed into the blood.
5. Blood takes nutrients to the liver. The liver turns some nutrients into sugar for energy.
6. The material that has gotten this far is waste. The large intestine sucks out water and minerals.
7. Finally, the solid waste leaves the body out the anus.

Waterworks

As your blood circulates through your body, it picks up waste materials from your other cells. This waste needs to constantly be removed. Two very efficient blood cleaners—your kidneys—do the job. Each is made up of millions of microscopic filters called **nephrons**. Waste materials and extra water filter out of the kidneys, down the ureters and into the bladder—ready to leave the body as urine.

The Urinary System

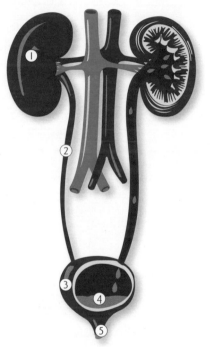

1. **kidney**
Each kidney makes up to 4 cups of urine a day!

2. **ureter**
The muscles in the walls of the ureters push the small amounts of urine to the bladder every 10 to 15 seconds.

3. **bladder**
Your bladder is about the size of a walnut when empty, but can stretch to hold about two cups of liquid.

4. **urine**
Urine contains water, ammonia, salts, urea (broken-down protein), and other waste products.

5. **urethra**
Urine leaves the body through this tube. A man's urethra is four times longer than a woman's.

Your kidneys filter all the blood in your body up to 350 times a day!

Water Watchers

Kidneys keep the level of water and minerals in your body balanced. If there is too little water in the blood, the brain tells the kidneys to make less urine. Too much water? The kidneys make more urine.

Life Goes On

Every living thing reproduces. Reproduction is how a species makes sure others of its kind continue to survive after the parents are gone. Humans begin life as a single cell. Where does this cell come from?

Women make egg cells in organs called ovaries, while men make sperm cells in their testicles. When a sperm meets an egg, the two come together to make a new cell called a **zygote**. The zygote has special information (called **genes**) from both parents. Genes control how we look—that's why a child often looks a lot like her parents. It takes about nine months for the zygote to gradually develop into a baby ready to enter the world!

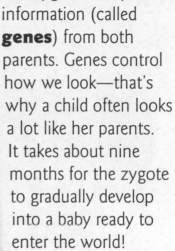

Double Take!

*If two eggs are **fertilized**, the mother will have twins. If one egg is fertilized, but splits into two zygotes, the mother will have identical twins that will be the same sex and look exactly alike!*

Reproductive System

A man's reproductive system is mostly outside his body, while a woman's is inside her abdomen.

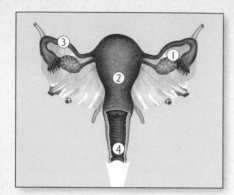

1. **ovary**
Every month, one egg (rarely more than one) leaves an ovary and enters the fallopian tube.

2. **uterus**
Usually the size of a small pear, the uterus can stretch to fit the growing baby!

3. **fallopian tube**
Tiny hairs (cilia) help move the egg to the uterus. The sperm meets the egg in the fallopian tube.

4. **vagina**
Sperm enters the body through the vagina. The vagina is also how the baby leaves the woman's body.

5. **penis**
6. **urethra**
Sperm and urine leave the man's body through this tube in the penis.

7. **scrotum**
The testicles are held in the scrotum outside the body where it is cooler. Sperm cells develop best below body temperature.

8. **testicle**
Millions of sperm are made in the two testicles every day!

9. **epididymis**
Sperm finish developing here and are stored until they are needed.

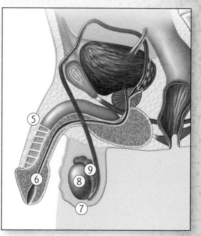

Eggscellent Ovaries!

A baby girl is born with all the egg cells she will ever have! They wait in her ovaries until she is old enough to have a baby.

Glossary

antibody: A protein that some white cells use to "mark" things that don't belong in the body (like viruses and bacteria). The antibody shows the immune system what needs to be destroyed.

bacteria: A one-celled living organism—sometimes called a germ. In large numbers, some can make people sick.

blood vessel: Tubes that transport the blood throughout the body. Arteries, veins, and capillaries are blood vessels.

cell: The smallest living thing. All living things are made of cells—from microscopic creatures to plants and animals.

cilia: Tiny hairs on the surface of some types of cells that wave back and forth. Cilia in the nose move dirt out of the body.

cochlea: The part of the ear that turns sound vibrations into nerve signals the brain can understand.

enamel: The outermost mineral layer on the teeth and the hardest material in the body.

enzyme: A protein that speeds up chemical reactions to make changes to a substance. Enzymes in the body break down food for digestion.

fertilize: The act of joining a sperm cell and egg cell to make a new cell that may grow into a baby.

fibrin: A stringlike protein that forms a kind of mesh in a wound. This mesh traps platelets to plug the wound and form a clot.

gene: The information in each cell that decides everything physical about you. Hair color, skin color, and height are all decided by genes.

germ: A virus, fungus, or bacteria that can cause illness in a living thing.

gland: An organ that makes and releases a substance the body can use. Some things glands make are hormones, sweat, and oil.

hemoglobin: An iron-containing pigment in red blood cells that gives them their color and carries oxygen.

hormone: A special chemical in the body that acts as a messenger to tell certain cells what to do.

insulin: A hormone made by the pancreas that helps cells absorb sugar from the blood to use for energy.

molecule: The smallest piece of material that a substance can be made of. There are billions of molecules in each cell.

mucous membrane: An area of very thin "skin" that makes mucus and is always moist. The inside of the mouth is made of mucous membranes.

mucus: A slimy material that is made in the body to help keep certain parts moist and protected.

nephrons: Tiny filters in the kidney that take waste materials out of the blood.

nutrient: A chemical that the body can use for energy, or for building or repairing tissues. Calcium is a nutrient.

organ: A collection of tissues that has a basic job to do. The heart, liver, brain, glands, and skin are examples of organs.

papillae: A "bump" that contains cells used for taste, smell, or touch. The papillae on the tongue have taste buds on them.

phagocytosis: A cell's process of "eating" a smaller cell or germ by surrounding and digesting it.

pigment: A substance that gives color to cells or tissues. Melanin is a pigment in the skin.

protein: A substance that makes up most of the material in the body. Skin, hair, hormones, enzymes, and antibodies are made of protein.

pulmonary: Something that has to do with the lungs. Pulmonary veins carry blood from the lungs into the heart.

retina: The inner surface of the eye that is sensitive to light.

saliva: A liquid made in the mouth that moistens food so that it can be swallowed. Saliva also starts to digest the food before it is swallowed.

tissue: A group of similar cells that forms a part of the body. Muscles are a type of tissue.

urine: The body's liquid waste that is made by the kidneys.

virus: A very simple organism that must enter the body's cells in order to make copies of itself. Viruses cause illness.

zygote: The new cell that is formed when a sperm and egg come together. The zygote gradually develops into a new person.

ART AND PHOTOGRAPH CREDITS

(t = top, b = bottom, l = left, r = right, c = center)

Cover: ©alxhar/ Shutterstock.com (l), ©Ramona Kaulitzki/Shutterstock.com (tr), ©Alila Sao Mai/Shutterstock.com (tl, bc, br), ©Sebastian Kaulitzki/Shutterstock.com (c), ©Germán Ariel Berra /Shutterstock.com (b); Back Cover: ©alxhar/ Shutterstock.com (tl, r), ©SergiyN/Shutterstock.com (tl), ©Alila Sao Mai/Shutterstock.com (tc), Shirley Beckes (tr, bl), Alila Sao Mai/Shutterstock.com (bc); Page 2: ©naluwan/Shutterstock.com; Title Page: ©Kruglov_Orda/Shutterstock.com; Page 4 ©SergiyN/Shutterstock.com (b), ©MedusArt/Shutterstock.com (b overlay); Page 5: ©jannoon028/Shutterstock.com (tl), ©Alila Sao Mai/Shutterstock.com (tr, b), ©Germán Ariel Berra/Shutterstock.com (br); Page 6: ©michaeljung/Shutterstock.com; Page 7: ©Ramona Kaulitzki/Shutterstock.com (ct), ©Alila Sao Mai/Shutterstock.com (c); Page 8: ©Anton BalazhShutterstock.com (c), Shirley Beckes (b); Page 9: ©Andrea Danti/Shutterstock.com; Page 10: ©MANDY GODBEHEAR/Shutterstock.com (t), ©Harm Kruyshaar/Shutterstock.com (c), Shirley Beckes (b); Page 11: ©Yuri Samsonov/Shutterstock.com (cl), ©Germán Ariel Berra /Shutterstock.com (c, cr), ©Afronova/Shutterstock.com (b); Page 12: ©Angela Hawkey/Shutterstock.com (cr), ©Orla/Shutterstock.com (cl), ©dayzeran/Shutterstock.com (b); Page 13: ©alxhar/Shutterstock.com (t); Page 14: ©Alila Sao Mai/Shutterstock.com (c), ©blessings/Shutterstock.com (b); Page 15: ©Kruglov_Orda/Shutterstock.com (c), ©itsmejust/Shutterstock.com (cl), ©Deckard_73/Shutterstock.com (cr), ©janoon028/Shutterstock.com (cr); Page 16: ©tankist276/Shutterstock.com (tr); Page 17: ©alxhar/Shutterstock.com (c), ©Blamb/Shutterstock.com (br); Page 18: ©leonello calvetti/Shutterstock.com (c), ©Anetta/Shutterstock.com (b); Page 19: ©Sofia Santos/Shutterstock.com (t), ©Yuri Arcurs/Shutterstock.com (cl, cc), ©Zurijeta/Shutterstock.com (cc), ©juan carlos tinjaca/Shutterstock.com (cl); Page 20: ©michaeljung/Shutterstock.com (t), ©Rob Dack/Shutterstock.com (b); Page 21: ©alxhar/Shutterstock.com (tl); Page 22: ©Sebastian Kaulitzki/Shutterstock.com (c), © Graça Victoria/Shutterstock.com (b); Page 23: ©SergiyN/Shutterstock.com (c), ©MedusArt/Shutterstock.com (c overlay); Page 24: ©kovacevic/Shutterstock.com (t), ©Lane V. Erickson/Shutterstock.com (b); Page 25: ©Oguz Aral/Shutterstock.com (t), ©AISPIX by Image Source/Shutterstock.com (b); Page 26: ©Gelpi/Shutterstock.com (t), ©Piotr Marcinski/Shutterstock.com (c), ©Nattika/Shutterstock.com (cl) ©Lev Kropotov/Shutterstock.com (cl) ©Rob Stark/Shutterstock.com (cr) ©Picsfive/Shutterstock.com (cr), ©David Davis/Shutterstock.com (b); Page 27: ©Petrenko Andriy/Shutterstock.com (t), ©Ogus Aral/iStockphoto.com (c), ©pdesign/Shutterstock.com (b); Page 28: ©Lightspring/ Shutterstock.com; Page 29: ©alxhar/Shutterstock.com (tl); Page 30: ©ancroft/Shutterstock.com (t), Yanas/Shutterstock.com (b); Page 31: ©Alila Sao Mai/Shutterstock.com; Page 32: ©MiAdS/Shutterstock.com (l), ©Ramona Kaulitzki/Shutterstock.com (t), ©pinkkoala/Shutterstock.com (br); Page 33: ©Melianiaka Kanstantsin/Shutterstock.com (t), ©Fedor Kondratenko/Shutterstock.com (b); Page 34: ©Thomas M Perkins/Shutterstock.com (t), ©Pakhnyushcha/Shutterstock.com (b), ©Elena Elisseeva/Shutterstock.com (b); Page 35: ©alxhar/Shutterstock.com (tr); Page 36: ©Gelpi/Shutterstock.com (c), ©Ken Hurst/Shutterstock.com; Page 37: ©alxhar/ Shutterstock.com; Page 38: ©Evgenia Sh./Shutterstock.com (tl), Page 39: ©alxhar/Shutterstock.com (c), ©Rob Wilson/Shutterstock.com (b); Page 40: ©Piotr Marcinski/Shutterstock.com; Page 41: ©ovii/Shutterstock.com (t), ©vasi2/Shutterstock.com (b); Page 42: ©Anneka/Shutterstock.com (c), ©Christopher Halloran/Shutterstock.com (b); Page 43: ©Alex Luengo/Shutterstock.com (t), ©Andrea Danti/Shutterstock.com (b); Page 45: ©blessings/Shutterstock.com

Body system cards: ©alxhar/ Shutterstock.com

Published by Reader's Digest Children's Books
44 South Broadway, White Plains, NY 10601 U.S.A. and
Reader's Digest Children's Publishing Limited,
The Ice House, 124-126 Walcot Street, Bath UK BA1 5BG
© 2013 Reader's Digest Children's Publishing, Inc.
All rights reserved. Reader's Digest and Reader's Digest Children's Books
are registered trademarks of The Reader's Digest Association, Inc.
Manufactured in China. Conforms to ASTM F963
10 9 8 7 6 5 4 3 2 1